A Glut of Apples & Pears

Ann Carr

Illustrated by
Martin MacKeown

MEREHURST PRESS
—LONDON—

*The Publishers wish to thank
Rosemary Wilkinson and Malcolm Saunders
for their help with this book.*

First published 1988 by Merehurst Press
5 Great James Street
London WC1N 3DA

Produced by
Malcolm Saunders Publishing Ltd
26 Ornan Road, London NW3 4QB

ISBN 0 948075 87 2

Photoset in Linotype Ehrhardt
by Fakenham Photosetting Limited
Printed in Spain

CONTENTS

FOREWORD

We are spoilt with apples. They are with us all the year round and from all over the world: red, green, yellow and russet, not to mention the golden variety. We have them on picnics, for school lunches, on buses and trains, for breakfast or supper – and everybody's fruitbowl has an apple. In fact, this fruit has become so common we treat it with less respect than that ground apple, the potato, and our beautiful home-produced apples lie rotting beneath the trees.

Fine apples and rare varieties fill orchards and gardens. We should use them, picking them from the trees or buying them in the markets, in order not to lose the wonderful old-fashioned varieties.

And what of pears? They, too, are available all year though not in such abundance and the glut season is short. Pears are a fragile fruit and need to be used up quickly, otherwise they will go 'dozy' or sleepy and tasteless.

The exciting and practical recipes in this book for both sweet and savoury dishes, will help you to use up your glut, be it of delicate pears or a whole apple tree laden with fruit.

INTRODUCTION

Apples and pears are both members of the family *rosaceae*, the rose family.

Unless you have an orchard or an apple or pear tree in your garden, you could easily be unaware of the seasonal surplus which these fruit trees produce, since we are so used to the year-round availability of these fruits in the shops and markets. But it is precisely because they do produce gluts that we can enjoy apples, if not pears, out of season. Their good keeping qualities have meant that when picked at their peak and correctly stored, they can be kept throughout the winter. This used to mean storing them in an airy loft, so that by early spring they had become wrinkled and flabby, but still much valued as the only fresh fruit available. Nowadays, we

11

can eat these fruits in remarkably good condition at any time thanks to the modern storage techniques, though these do little for the flavour of the already rather flavourless modern apple.

Apple cultivation is so old nobody can accurately date when or where it started and there are now far too many varieties to be recorded, though, sadly, the choice in shops and markets is limited. Old-fashioned varieties may be hard to find but are worth hunting for as apples to eat and especially if you are about to plant trees.

Apple trees like a well-drained soil and an airy, sunny position. Slightly sloping land is ideal. Apart from careful pruning during the first five years and weed clearance at the base

of the trunk, the trees need little attention. They are rewarding to grow for in most years the tree will crop well. It is best to seek specialist help on which trees are most suited to your area and which of the old-fashioned varieties are still available.

One tree can produce a big enough glut for a family to cope with but the world's average annual crop is a staggering forty seven thousand million pounds or twenty one thousand million kilogrammes. Six thousand million pounds of these are produced in the U.S.A. and about four thousand million pounds in Europe. Both Australia and New Zealand are now important producers and exporters.

Shop and market gluts will probably be of the most common commercial varieties: Bramley seedlings for cooking and Golden

Delicious, Red Delicious, Jonathans, Coxes, Granny Smiths and Russets for eaters.

The pear tree produces one of the world's most important and beautiful fruits. It is not generally known that its commercial value exceeds that of the peach, plum or cherry. The success of the commercial crop of the apple has overshadowed that of the subtle-flavoured pear. Oval and narrower at one end than the other, it comes in many lovely colours: from delicate shades of green to yellow and dull gold tinged with orange. The best fruits are scented and succulent with a hint of grainy grittiness in the texture of the flesh. Hard pears for cooking are often dry and

very gritty but bite into a perfect, ripe pear and the juice will instantly ooze from the soft flesh.

Dessert pears are a delicate fruit: they bruise easily and need handling with care. If you can't pick straight from the tree for immediate consumption, dessert or eating pears are best picked under-ripe and kept in an even temperature to ripen. Pears for sale commercially are always picked unripe to prevent too much bruising, though it is thought that this might result in a dead flavour and 'pappy' texture.

The finest dessert pears, such as the aromatic Williams, can reach their peak of perfection in two to five hours after picking.

These are the pears that flavour the famous eau-de-vie de *Poire William*, which is so popular in Alsace and Switzerland. The rather more humble perry, a sort of pear cider is also made with dessert pears.

Pears have been regarded as a poor substitute for the apple; this unfair reputation for one of the world's supreme fruits may perhaps have developed for two very good reasons: commercially and financially pears are a difficult crop and their subtle delicate flavour is lost if the fruit is bruised, so that few people have ever tasted a pear at its finest.

By comparison with apples, the world's production of pears is small: a mere fifteen

thousand million pounds or seven thousand million kilogrammes, half of which is produced in Europe. Again, compared with apples, the pear varieties are few, running only to hundreds, rather than thousands. In America, Canada and Australia, half the crop goes straight into cans, especially the famous Bartlett pears which can so well.

Pear trees, like apple trees, require a well-drained soil. They also need a sunny, sheltered position and grow particularly well on a south-facing wall where they can be elegantly espaliered. The trees will need pruning for they can reach a height of 40 feet (13 metres) if neglected. As with apples, when planting new trees it is best to seek advice from local growers as to what would best suit your soil and climate.

The most common varieties are Comice, Conference, Josephine de Malines, Williams' (short for Williams' Bon Chrétien) and the Australian Packham.

The juicy pear Lies, in a soft profusion, scattered round.

(1730, Thomson, Autumn)

COOKS' NOTES

1. Unless specific details are given in the individual recipes, the following apply:
– spoon measurements are level
– sugar is granulated
– eggs are standard size
2. Follow either the imperial measurements or the metric but do not mix them, as they have been calculated separately.
3. As individual oven temperatures vary, use the timings in the recipes as a guide. Always preheat your oven or grill.

The
Recipes

APPLES

The results of cooking with apples will depend on the flavour of the raw apple: the better this is, the better the finished dish will be. However, cooking with the help of butter, sugar, herbs or spices can greatly enhance a bland apple and for this reason alone it is worth cooking them.

For dishes such as tarts, pies, flans and apple cakes, eaters are preferable to cookers, since the apple slices are more likely to remain whole. Cookers tend to break down to a soft pulp.

A short list of eating apples most likely to be available may be useful when using up a bargain-priced glut in local shops or supermarkets. Beauty of Bath and the Australian Rome Beauty are blush-red and yellow, smooth-skinned and slightly tart; they have plenty of flavour and stew well. Discovery and Worcester Pearmaine are both smooth-skinned and turn shiny red. They are soft-textured and hold their shape when cooked. Next come the Coxes, Laxtons, Sturmers, Russets and Rennets, famous for their fine flavour, excellent for eating and splendid to cook with. Their skins are often slightly rough and their colour ranging from russet through orange to dull red.

Granny Smith is a hard, green, crisp apple available with imports all year round, as are Red Delicious, Starkings and Jonathans. Their colours range from yellow, green and red to a yellow and red-striped Jonathan. All are eaters but make good cooking apples, especially the Granny Smith, which can replace the Bramley.

Cookers tend to be large, hard, green and tart. During cooking they turn to a soft pulp but with their skins left on are our most popular apple for baking: a great pity, for a baked sweet, flavoursome eater is quite a different experience – try it! Cookers are also the apples used to complement savoury dishes, particularly fatty or rich meat and poultry, such as pork or goose. Bramley is the most renowned of the cookers.

Chyldren loue an apple more than golde.
(1398, Trevisa)

Apple & Celeriac Soup

A homely, comforting winter soup using up windfalls: cookers or eaters will do.

Serves 6–8

2 oz (60 g) butter

1 head celeriac, peeled and cut into 1 1/2 in (4 cm) cubes

1 medium onion, peeled and chopped

4 apples, peeled and chopped

30 fl oz (940 ml) stock

20–30 fl oz (625–940 ml) milk

salt and pepper, to taste

Melt 1 oz (30 g) butter in a large saucepan with a tight-fitting lid, then add celeriac, onion and apples and stir-fry for 5 to 10 minutes, until vegetables are just beginning to colour. Add stock, cover and simmer for 3/4 to 1 hour. Strain off stock and reserve, then purée vegetables and apples in a blender or food processor. Return to pan, add stock, milk, salt and pepper. To finish, add remaining butter, stir well and serve at once.

Pork & Apple Terrine

For this recipe use eating apples: cookers would be too mushy.

Serves 6
2 onions, finely chopped
1½ lb (750 g) lean pork, finely chopped
2 oz (60 g) back fat, finely chopped
2 oz (60 g) fat bacon, finely chopped
2 teaspoons chopped fresh lemon thyme
2 sage leaves, chopped
2 teaspoons grated lemon peel
salt and freshly ground black pepper, to taste
20 fl oz (625 ml) dry cider
1 tablespoon cider vinegar
4 eating apples
3 hard-boiled eggs

Place first 8 ingredients in a bowl. Beat together cider and cider vinegar, then pour over ingredients in bowl. Mix well, cover and leave in a cool place or the fridge to marinate overnight.

Next day strain off liquid and reserve. Peel, core and roughly chop apples, shell and chop eggs – they should look like rather coarse breadcrumbs. Layer pork mixture, apple and eggs in a 2½ pint (1.5 litre) terrine or loaf tin, starting and finishing with a layer of meat. Pour over reserved juices, cover with foil, stand the dish in a baking tin of cold water and bake in a moderate oven at 180 °C (350 °F/Gas 4) for 1½ to 2 hours, removing foil 30 minutes before end of cooking time.

Remove from oven, replace foil and weight lightly overnight – 12 to 16 oz (375 to 500 g) pressure. If, when you remove terrine from oven, there seems to be a lot of juice, strain off a little, but be careful as the juice will keep the terrine moist.

Beetroot Relish

This recipe was given to me by my hostess at a lunch party some time ago. She had been making it for years but I have never come across it since and although we love it, I only make it once a year, at Christmas, to serve with cold meats and left-over turkey.

1 medium-sized cooked beetroot
2 eating apples
2 teaspoons grated onion
1 tablespoon sugar
2 tablespoons wine vinegar
1/2 grated nutmeg (use less if you prefer)
salt and pepper, to taste

Place all the ingredients in a blender or food processor and purée until smooth. Serve as a relish with hot or cold meats.

This keeps for 3 to 4 weeks, covered, in the fridge, but the nutmeg flavour intensifies.

Cabbage & Apples

This is good made with the dark green cabbages known as Savoys.

Serves 6–8

1 cabbage, chopped

2 cooking or dessert apples, peeled and chopped

2 spring onions, chopped or ½ onion, chopped and fried in a little butter

2 oz (60 g) butter

salt and pepper, to taste

Parboil cabbage in a saucepan with a tight-fitting lid for about 10 minutes. Drain well, chop and return to pan. Add apples, onion, butter, salt and pepper, cover and cook for a further 10 minutes over a very low heat, watching carefully to make sure cabbage doesn't stick and burn. Savoy cabbages may take longer to cook than the large, hard, white variety. They should still be a little crunchy when finished.

Poached Whole Apples as a Vegetable

These make an excellent vegetable to accompany pork or bacon, goose or game.

Make a sugar syrup by dissolving 2–4 oz (60–125 g) sugar in 20 fl oz (625 ml) water, flavoured with the pared peel of 1 lemon and 3 cloves. When dissolved, boil for 10 minutes until thickened. Peel and core some apples, they should be a variety that will not disintegrate easily in cooking, then poach in the syrup over a gentle heat, until just tender, 20 to 30 minutes depending on size.

You can finish these off by frying them in some bacon fat or serve them as they are, sprinkled with chopped parsley and chives.

As the apple tree among the trees of the wood, so is my beloved among the sons. I sat down under his shadow with great delight and his fruit was sweet to my taste.

(Song of Solomon)

Haricot Beans with Apples

A German dish which is wholesome and good; the apples seem to take away the 'windyness' that dried pulses often leave and which spoils them for many people. Served with a carrot salad this makes a nice winter supper.

Serves 4

8 oz (250 g) white haricot beans

4 oz (125 g) streaky bacon, rinds removed and reserved, meat chopped

2 oz (60 g) butter

2 onions, finely chopped

1 lb (500 g) apples, peeled, cored and sliced

1 tablespoon brown sugar

pinch ground cloves

salt and pepper, to taste

Soak beans overnight in plenty of cold water, they swell quite a lot. Cook in plenty of fresh

30

water until tender, 1 to 1½ hours. After about 40 minutes, add bacon rinds, then prepare remaining ingredients.

Melt butter in a saucepan, add onions and fry gently for 10 to 15 minutes until really tender. Add bacon, apples, sugar and cloves, cover and simmer for 15 to 20 minutes, until apples are soft and beginning to go mushy. If more moisture is needed during the cooking, add 1 to 2 tablespoons of the liquid in which beans are cooking. When beans are tender, drain, place in a serving dish and pour over apple and bacon sauce. Add salt and pepper and mix gently.

Rough tasted appules are holsome where the stomake is weake.

(1533, Elyot)

Savoury Stuffed Apples from the Levant

This Middle-Eastern dish makes an unusual alternative to stuffed tomatoes or peppers.

Serves 4
4 large cooking apples
3 oz (90 g) butter
1 small onion, chopped
1 clove garlic, chopped
1 teaspoon cinnamon
$^1/_2$ teaspoon ground allspice
$^1/_2$ teaspoon ground ginger
2 teaspoons chopped fresh mint
2 oz (60 g) walnuts, chopped
2 oz (60 g) currants, cleaned
8 oz (250 g) cooked minced lamb
salt and pepper, to taste
2–4 tablespoons water
plain boiled rice, to serve

Wipe apples clean, remove core, making a large hole but be careful not to break apples. Melt 2 oz (60 g) of the butter in a frying pan, add onion and garlic and fry gently for 7 to 8 minutes until tender, then add spices and fry for a further 2 minutes. Remove from heat and add mint, walnuts, currants, lamb, salt and pepper. Mix with the hands to a smooth, stiff paste, then use to stuff apples. Pour water into a shallow ovenproof dish to just

cover the bottom. Stand apples in dish, divide remaining butter into four and place one portion on top of each apple. Cover the top of each apple with a small piece of foil to prevent stuffing from burning. You may like also to cut a ring round the waist of each apple to allow for expansion, rather than letting them burst due to overcooking. Place in oven and bake at 190 °C (375 °F/Gas 5) for 30 to 35 minutes, then serve with plain boiled rice.

Names quite as inseparable as goose and apple-sauce.

(1824, Miss Mitford)

Horseradish Sauce with Apple

This is good with hot or cold meats and with fish. It can be served hot or cold and will keep, covered, in the fridge for 6 to 8 weeks.

2 oz (60 g) butter
1 lb (500 g) apples, peeled and cored
pinch nutmeg
2 teaspoons grated horseradish
3 tablespoons brandy
1–2 teaspoons sugar
salt and pepper, to taste

Melt butter in a saucepan and add apples, spice and horseradish. Cover and simmer over a low heat until very soft – 10 to 20 minutes, depending on apples (cookers take less time than eaters), then purée in a blender or food processor. Stir in brandy, followed by sugar, salt and pepper to taste.

Apple & Bacon Supper

Quick, simple and delicious.

Serves 4

12 oz (375 g) streaky bacon

*3–4 apples, peeled, cored, sliced and
parboiled for 5 minutes*

*4–6 oz (125–185 g) hard cheese,
Cheddar is good*

Trim rinds and boney pieces from bacon, drain apples and pat dry, slice cheese into small fingers about ¼ in (0.5 cm) thick. Lay some cheese and one or two apple slices on each piece of bacon, roll up and place, join down, in a baking tin. Bake at 190 °C (375 °F/Gas 5) for 10 minutes or until bacon is cooked and cheese runs.

Serve with a dish or mashed potatoes or a favourite cabbage dish.

Apple & Sausage Layer

This is a popular children's supper. It is simply two layers of sausage meat with a fat layer of peeled, cored and chopped apples in between. For 3 to 4 people, use 1 lb (500 g) sausage meat and 8 oz (250 g) apples and place in an ovenproof dish with some spices or herbs, such as sage. Bake at 190°C (375°F/Gas 5) for 20 to 25 minutes until top is crisp and apples are cooked. Serve with potatoes baked in their jackets.

A plump, rosy-cheeked, apple-faced young woman.

(1848, Dickens, Dombey & Son)

Apple & Bacon Burgers

This is another children's favourite and good for using up left-over potatoes.

Serves 2–4
1 oz (30 g) butter
1/2 onion, chopped
3–4 cold cooked potatoes, mashed
2 apples, peeled, cored and chopped
4 rashers bacon, chopped or equivalent of bacon pieces
salt and pepper, to taste
1/2–1 egg, beaten
4 tablespoons cooking oil

Melt butter in a frying pan and gently fry onion until tender but not coloured, 5 to 10 minutes. Place in a bowl with mashed potato and stir in apple, bacon, salt and pepper and enough beaten egg to bind mixture together. Form into patties, heat oil in a frying pan and fry patties gently on both sides until golden. Serve at once.

Savoury Apple Pancakes

Make pancakes following recipe on page 84
and keep warm while preparing the following
filling.

Serves 6
1 oz (30 g) butter
1/2 onion, finely chopped
1 apple, peeled and finely chopped
8 oz (250 g) cold cooked chicken, cubed
1/2 teaspoon curry paste or 1 teaspoon
curry powder
8 oz (250 g) Greek-style yogurt
1 teaspoon sugar
salt and pepper, to taste

Melt butter in a saucepan, add onion and
apple and cook until tender, about 5 minutes.
Stir in chicken, curry paste or powder, 1
tablespoon of the yogurt, sugar, salt and pepper. Mix well and continue cooking until
heated through. Fill pancakes and serve with
rest of yogurt in a bowl.

Savoury Apple Dumplings

A cheese sauce would make a good accompaniment to these dumplings.

Serves 4

2 oz (60 g) butter

*6–8 oz (185–250 g) lean cooked ham,
chopped*

*2 spring onions, green and white parts
chopped*

salt and pepper, to taste

8 oz (250 g) Suet Pastry (see page 84)

4 medium apples, not too tart

Mix butter, ham, spring onions, salt and pepper together well in a bowl. Roll out pastry and cut into 4 squares large enough to wrap round apples. Peel apples and core without breaking, then place one on each square of pastry. Fill centre of each apple with ham and onion stuffing, then draw up pastry round apples, damping the 4 corners well and pinching them together at the top of the apples. Traditionally these dumplings were wrapped in well-floured cloths and boiled but it is easier to wrap them in foil and steam for 1 hour.

A word aptly spoken is like apples of gold in pictures of silver.

(The Book of Proverbs)

Sage Pudding

A very old recipe adapted from an early 18th century diary. It is a filling dish and, omitting the bacon, would make a good vegetarian supper.

Serves 4

2 oz (60 g) butter

1 onion, chopped

4 hard-boiled eggs, very finely chopped

3 oz (90 g) breadcrumbs

6 oz (185 g) streaky bacon, rinds removed and chopped

4 sage leaves, chopped

salt and pepper, to taste

3 eggs, beaten

3–4 fl oz (90–125 ml) milk

4 apples, peeled and sliced

Melt butter in a frying pan, add onion and fry gently for 8 to 10 minutes, do not allow to brown. Place hard-boiled eggs, bread-crumbs, bacon and sage leaves in a mixing bowl, add cooked onions, salt and pepper, then pour on beaten eggs and enough milk to give a soft dropping consistency. Turn mixture into a well-buttered ovenproof dish, cover with apples, brush with milk and bake at 190 °C (375 °F/Gas 5) for 30 to 40 minutes. The top should be deep, golden-brown and the pudding firm but not dry.

Your argument is as like, as an apple is like an oyster.

(1579, Fulke)

Apple & Potato Fidget

Serves 4
1½ lb (750 g) potatoes, peeled
4–5 oz (125–155 g) butter
2 onions, chopped
3 cooking apples, peeled and quartered
1 tablespoon capers
4 anchovy fillets, chopped, if desired
6 fl oz (185 ml) cider
salt and pepper, to taste

Boil potatoes in a pan until almost cooked. Cool and slice thickly. Place in an ovenproof dish. Melt butter in a frying pan, add onions and fry gently until cooked, do not brown. Remove from pan and add to potatoes. In the same pan, fry apples until almost cooked, add to potato mixture together with capers, anchovy, cider, salt and pepper. Cover with foil and bake in a hot oven, 190 °C (375 °F/ Gas 5) for 7 to 10 minutes, until heated through.

41

Meatballs & Apple Sauce

The sauce can be prepared 2 to 3 days in advance, covered and stored in the fridge.

Serves 4

1 lb (500 g) cooking apples, peeled, cored and sliced

3 oz (90 g) butter

1½ teaspoons chopped fresh sage

1 oz (30 g) sugar

salt and pepper, to taste

½ medium onion, chopped

1 lb (500 g) beef, pork or poultry, very finely minced

2 oz (60 g) breadcrumbs

1 egg, beaten

1–2 tablespoons milk, if required

4–6 tablespoons oil, for frying

To make the sauce, place apples, 2 oz (60 g) butter and 1 teaspoon sage in a heavy pan

with a tight-fitting lid. Cover and cook over a gentle heat for 20 to 25 minutes until apples are soft and mushy, take care not to burn. Remove from heat, mash with a fork or beat with a wooden spoon, then add sugar, salt and pepper.

To make the meatballs, melt remaining butter in a frying pan and fry onion for a few minutes until transparent. Transfer to a bowl and add mincemeat, breadcrumbs, egg, remaining sage, salt and pepper. Knead mixture well together to make a smooth paste, adding a little milk if stiff, then, with floured hands, take walnut-sized pieces and quickly roll into balls. Alternatively, if time is short, divide mixture and shape into rissoles or sausages.

Heat oil and fry gently until brown all over and cooked through, 5 to 7 minutes for meatballs. Place on a serving dish and hand sauce separately.

Pork & Apple Pie

A useful pie which uses up cold, cooked pork. The quantities given are guidelines to serve 4 people. You can use more or less but keep the meat and apples roughly equal; all you need to remember is to use a deeper pie dish if you increase the amounts, the pastry should stretch.

1–1½ lb (500–750 g) apples, peeled, cored and chopped

1–1½ lb (500–750 g) cold pork, chopped

8–10 prunes, chopped

pinch cloves

pinch nutmeg

salt and pepper, to taste

2–4 fl oz (60–125 ml) dry cider

8 oz (250 g) Shortcrust Pastry (see page 82)

milk, for brushing

Layer apples with meat and prunes in an ovenproof pie dish just big enough to take them; this pie is best if packed really tightly beneath the pastry lid. Sprinkle over spices, salt and pepper, then pour over cider. Roll out pastry to fit dish, use to cover, brush with milk and bake at 190 °C (375 °F/Gas 5) for 30 to 40 minutes until golden brown.

A goodly apple rotten at the heart.
      (1596, Shakespeare, Merchant of Venice)

Apple & Pheasant Casserole

A variation of the classic dish often called Normandy Pheasant, as it is common in that part of France and indeed is popular throughout all northern France.

Serves 4

1 oz (30 g) butter

1 pheasant

1 lb (500 g) onions, peeled and sliced

1 lb (500 g) apples, peeled, cored and sliced

6 fl oz (185 ml) dry cider

2 tablespoons brandy

$^{1}/_{2}$ teaspoon ground cinnamon

$^{1}/_{4}$–$^{1}/_{2}$ teaspoon ground ginger

salt and pepper, to taste

Melt butter in a flameproof casserole with a tight-fitting lid. Add pheasant and brown all over. Remove bird, add onions and stir to coat well, then stir in apples, liquids, spices, salt and pepper. Lay pheasant carefully on top of these ingredients, cover and cook gently over a low heat for 1 hour or place in the oven and cook at 140 °C (275 °F/Gas 1) for 1 to 1½ hours until tender.

Remove bird from pan and keep warm.

Transfer onions and apple to a blender or food processor and purée. Skim off any fat from the pan juices, then add them to purée. If more liquid is needed to give a pouring consistency, deglaze the pan with more cider or a little stock and add. Serve purée with pheasant.

A Dish of Stewed Apples

So often tart and dull, these are wonderfully succulent and scented with rose water.

Take some sharp eating apples – 1–2 lb (500 g–1 kg) – peel, core and slice thinly, then just cover with water in a shallow pan. Add a walnut-sized knob of butter, bring them to the boil, cover and simmer until tender, stirring gently once or twice during the cooking. This should take 10 to 15 minutes, depending on the type of apples used, it doesn't spoil the dish if the apples break up. Now stir in 1–2 tablespoons rose water and 3–4 tablespoons of caster sugar. Turn into a serving dish and serve cold. As this is an old-fashioned dish, junket is the perfect accompaniment.

Little King Pippin
He built a fine hall,
Pie crust and pastry crust,
That was the wall.

(Nursery Rhyme)

Apple Bake
Serves 6
3 oz (90 g) breadcrumbs
4 oz (125 g) brown sugar
6 apples, peeled, cored and sliced
3 oz (90 g) butter
2 eggs, beaten
3 fl oz (90 ml) rum, brandy or calvados
double or whipping cream, whipped, to serve

Butter a 2 pint (1.25 litre) pie dish. Mix together breadcrumbs and sugar. Spread half the apples in the bottom of the pie dish, sprinkle with half the crumb and sugar mixture, then repeat with remaining apples and breadcrumbs. Melt butter in a saucepan and cool slightly. Beat eggs and spirit together, then stir in butter and pour over apple mixture. Bake at 180 °C (350 °F/Gas 4) for 30 to 40 minutes until golden brown on top and firm all through. Eat hot or warm, served with whipped cream.

Honey & Apple Bake

This is another version of the above recipe. Butter an ovenproof pie dish and layer with 4–6 sliced apples and 4–6 oz (125–185 g) biscuit crumbs. Spoon over 2 tablespoons clear honey and pour over 4 eggs beaten together with 6 fl oz (185 ml) single (light) cream. Bake as above.

Buttered Apples

This simple recipe is another French classic, although I have only eaten it at my own table and used to think it an invention from our own kitchen. Use your favourite eating apples. You need one apple per person; ½ oz (15 g) butter and 1 teaspoon caster or brown sugar per apple. (For the classic recipe we prefer brown sugar.)

Peel, core and slice each apple into about 8 pieces. Gently melt the butter in a heavy frying pan, add a layer of apples and cook until pale golden underneath. Turn and cook the other side, adding the sugar as you do so. You should end up with a delicious dish of just crunchy apples in their own caramel sauce. If you are cooking for several people, cook the apples in batches and keep the un-cooked slices white by dropping them into lightly salted water, but dry well before frying and keep warm when cooked.

The juice of Apples likewise, as of pippins, and pearemaines is of very good use in Melancholicke disease, helping to procure mirth, and to expell heavinesse.

The distilled water of the same Apples is of like effect.

(John Parkinson)

Sweet Apple Dumplings
Serves 4

1¹/₂ oz (45 g) butter, softened
2 oz (60 g) ground almonds
1 oz (30 g) mixed peel, very finely chopped
1 oz (30 g) caster sugar
2 teaspoons rose water
8 oz (250 g) puff pastry or Rough Puff
Pastry, see page 83
4 dessert apples
single (light) cream or custard, to serve

Place butter, almonds, mixed peel, sugar and rose water in a bowl and mix well together. Roll out pastry and cut into 4 squares large enough to wrap round apples. Peel and core apples. Place one on each square of pastry and fill centres with almond mixture, pressing well in. It doesn't matter if stuffing overflows. Damp the edges of the pastry, draw up corners and pinch firmly together.

Place on a buttered baking sheet and bake at 190°C (375°F/Gas 5) for 30 to 40 minutes or until golden. Eat while still warm with single cream or a real, old-fashioned pouring custard.

Faith, (as you say) there's small choise in rotten apples.
(1596, Shakespeare, The Taming of the Shrew)

*Of a wavering and fickle mind; as we say of
children; won with an apple, and lost with a nut.*
(1603, Sanderson, Sermons)

Old-Fashioned Apple Cake

This is delicious hot or cold as a pudding. It's
very good with sour cream poured over and
dusted with brown sugar.

Serves 4
2 tablespoons cake or biscuit crumbs
8 full-flavoured eating apples
2 tablespoons white wine
1 1/2 oz (45 g) butter
6 eggs
2 tablespoons sugar
1 teaspoon vanilla extract
1 teaspoon grated orange peel

Grease an 8 inch (20 cm) cake tin and dust
with crumbs. Peel and core apples. Place in a
pan with wine and butter, cover tightly and
cook until tender. Beat well and leave to cool.
Break eggs into a bowl, add sugar, vanilla and
orange peel and beat well. Fold into apple
mixture and pour into prepared cake tin.
Place tin in a pan of cold water and bake for
50 minutes at 190 °C (375 °F/Gas 5). Leave
to cool, then turn out and serve warm or cold.

Cider & Apple Preserve or Jelly

This is really an apple jelly, which is good with cold meats or game. The recipe comes from a daughter-in-law.

4 lb (2 kg) tart apples, windfalls are good
40 fl oz (1.25 litres) dry cider
2 in (5 cm) piece of cinnamon stick
4 cloves
1 lb (500 g) sugar to every 20 fl oz
(625 ml) liquid

Wash apples, remove blemishes and roughly chop. Do not peel or core. Place in a large pan with a tight-fitting lid, pour over cider, stir in spices and over a low heat bring to the boil. Reduce heat, cover and simmer very gently for 1 to 1½ hours. Pour into a jelly bag and leave to strain overnight.

Measure liquid and to every 20 fl oz (625 ml) add 1 lb (500 g) sugar. Transfer to the pan and bring gently to the boil, continue at a rolling boil until setting point is reached (see page 87). Take care not to overboil as this sets very easily. Pot and cover in the usual way (see page 87). Store in a cool, dark place.

Stay me with flagons, comfort me with apples: for I am sick of love.

(Song of Solomon)

Rosemary Apple Jelly

Excellent with lamb and game, this makes a change from the usual mint jelly.

3 lb (1.5 kg) cooking apples or windfalls
thinly pared peel of 1 orange
2 large sprigs of rosemary
40 fl oz (1.25 litres) water
1 lb (500 g) sugar to every 20 fl oz
(625 ml) juice

Wipe or wash and cut up apples, do not peel or core. Place in a large pan, add orange peel and rosemary, pour over water and bring to the boil, then simmer gently for ¾ to 1 hour until fruit is very soft and mushy. Strain through a jelly bag overnight.

Next day measure juice into the pan and add corresponding amount of sugar, bring slowly to the boil, stirring all the time, then boil hard for 5 to 10 minutes or until setting point is reached (see page 87). Skim off any scum, then leave to cool slightly before potting (see page 87). Store on a cool, dry shelf.

Appeles and peres that semen very gode,
Ful ofte tyme are roten by the core.
(c. 1430, John Lydgate)

Hot Apple Toddy

Serves 4
2 apples
2 tablespoons honey
20 fl oz (625 ml) cider
6 fl oz (185 ml) orange juice
pinch ground cloves, if desired
6 fl oz (185 ml) Calvados—brandy would
do

Wipe apples, remove cores and slice into rings. Heat honey in a pan, add apple rings and cook gently for 2 to 3 minutes. Pour on cider and orange juice, add cloves, if desired, and bring almost to boiling point. Stir in Calvados or brandy and serve at once, with apple rings.

PEARS

Without doubt, the finest pears are those from your own garden: sweet and scented, firm yet succulent and tender with the merest hint of sharpness to lift their flavour and quicken the palate. These wonders are best eaten straight from the tree if you are lucky enough to have access to one.

Pears, like apples, are divided into cookers and eaters. The Comice is a popular cooking variety. It has a dark green to russet, slightly rough skin. When cut, its firm hard flesh has a hint of pale green. It needs careful cooking for, if over-cooked, it takes on a greyish hue. Wardens are a superb cooking pear, which, if you can find them, cook to a delicate pink.

As so few varieties of cooking pears are available in our shops and markets, make use of the annual glut of home-grown dessert pears, such as Conference, Williams, Beurre Hardy, Beurre Bosc or Packham.

Choose firm, under-ripe pears without blemishes. A good eater will give a lot more flavour to the dish and be better value than a hard, mediocre cooking pear. In a time of glut, use the eaters generously.

Carrot, Pear & Almond Starter

Serves 4

*1 spring onion, white and green parts
chopped*

2 carrots, peeled and finely grated

2 pears, peeled and sliced

2 tablespoons sliced almonds, toasted

4 fl oz (125 ml) well-flavoured vinaigrette

Place all ingredients in a bowl, toss well to
mix and serve at once.

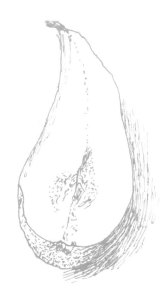

Pear & Watercress Salad

This makes a refreshing starter.

Serves 4

juice of 1 orange

juice of 1 lemon

*4 fl oz (125 ml) best nut oil, either
hazelnut or walnut*

salt and pepper, to taste

4 pears

1 bunch watercress, carefully sorted

*1 tangerine, clementine or satsuma, peeled
and segmented, to garnish*

*pumpernickel or brown bread and butter,
to serve*

Mix together fruit juices, oil, salt and pepper.
Peel and slice pears and place at once in
vinaigrette. Toss very gently and leave to
marinate for 20 to 30 minutes. Add watercress and mix gently but thoroughly. Garnish
with orange segments. Serve with slices of
bread and butter.

*Pear-stocks may also be raised of Suckers, but
those that are raised of Seeds or Stones are
esteemed much better.*

(1707, Mortimer)

Pears with Cheese & Walnuts

For each person you will need:

2 teaspoons cream cheese
1 teaspoon roughly chopped walnuts
salt and pepper, to taste
1 pear

SAUCE (for 4)
6 fl oz (185 ml) sour cream
1 tablespoon chopped fresh parsley
1 tablespoon chopped fresh chives
1/2 teaspoon finely chopped walnuts

First prepare the filling. Mix together cream cheese, walnuts, salt and pepper. Peel and halve pears, remove cores and stuff with cheese mixture. Place stuffing side down on individual plates. Mix cream and herbs thoroughly and spoon over and round pears. Dust with walnuts and serve.

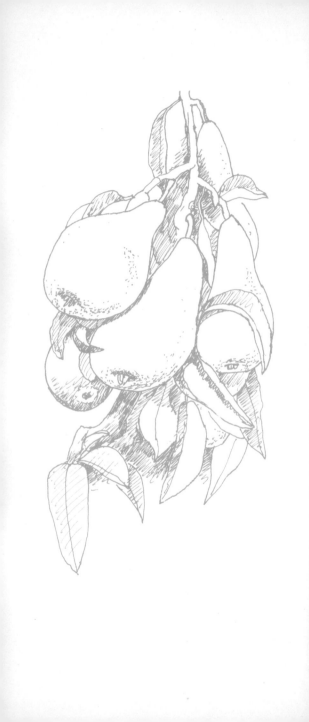

Leek & Pear Starter

This is a marvellous combination; good on its own or to accompany ham, pork or smoked chicken.

Serves 4

2 leeks

4 tablespoons olive oil

2 tablespoons lemon juice

1 teaspoon grated lemon peel

pinch ground mace

4 pears, peeled and cut into 1 in (2.5 cm) cubes

salt and pepper, to taste

1 tablespoon chopped fresh tarragon

2 teaspoons chopped fresh chives or spring onion greens

Trim and wash leeks well, dry thoroughly on absorbent kitchen paper, then slice into rings not more than ¼ in (0.5 cm) thick. Pour olive oil into a shallow pan with a tight-fitting lid and heat gently, then add leeks, cover and sweat for 5 minutes. Add lemon juice and peel, mace and pears, cover again and sweat for a further 5 minutes. Remove from heat and, still covered, leave to cool. To serve, sprinkle with salt and pepper and garnish with tarragon and chives or spring onions.

Take PereWardonys, and sethe hem in Wyne.
(c. 1430, Two Cookery-books)

Sweet & Sour Pear Sauce

Good with roast pork or game, as well as with shoulder of lamb.

2 teaspoons cooking oil
2 spring onions, chopped
2 pears, peeled, cored and chopped
2 teaspoons chopped preserved ginger
6 fl oz (185 ml) cider
2 teaspoons cornflour
2 teaspoons vinegar
2 teaspoons sugar
1 cardamom pod, seeds removed and lightly crushed
salt and pepper, to taste

Heat oil in a frying pan, add onions, pears and ginger and stir-fry for 5 minutes. Use a little of the cider to make a paste with cornflour before adding rest of cider, vinegar, sugar, cardamom seeds, salt and pepper. Pour over ingredients in pan and bring to the boil, stirring constantly. Continue boiling until mixture thickens and becomes clear: it should be the consistency of thick cream.

'But is the pear ripe?' said the diplomatist. 'The pear is ripe if we have the courage to pluck it', said Lord Marney.

(1845, Sybil Disraeli)

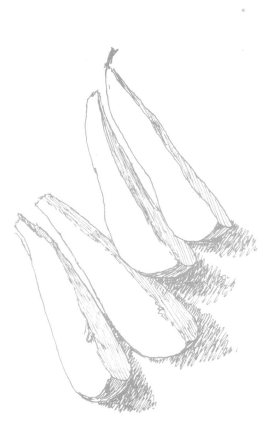

Pears with Green Beans

When your palate is tired of plain beans at the end of the season, try adding some ripe, peeled and chopped pear and a nut of butter to the beans. Finish off with a few chopped, toasted almonds and some freshly ground black pepper.

Pears with Walnut Sauce

This is an unusual combination but very delicious. A contrast in texture and colour is needed with this dish: really good black olives are wonderful.

Poach some pears in a little water to which you have added 1 tablespoon vinegar, 1 blade mace, 1 slice orange, 2 cloves, 1 teaspoon sugar and salt and pepper to taste. Do not overcook the fruit, they should still be firm. Remove from liquid and keep warm at the side of the cooker or, covered, in the oven while you make the following sauce, which will serve 4 to 6.

2 slices white bread, crusts removed
4–6 tablespoons milk
2 oz (60 g) butter, melted
1 stick celery, very finely chopped
1 clove garlic, crushed
4 oz (125 g) walnuts, ground
6 fl oz (185 ml) Greek-style yogurt
salt and pepper, to taste

Soak bread in milk, then mash well together and set aside. Melt butter in a small saucepan, add celery and cook gently for 3 to 5 minutes, do not allow to brown. Add garlic and cook for a further 2 to 3 minutes, then add walnuts, yogurt, bread mixture, salt and pepper. Heat gently and serve at once with the pears.

Roast Chicken with Pears

This is a pot roast to serve 5 to 6 people.

In a large flameproof casserole with a tight-fitting lid heat 2 tablespoons cooking oil. Add 2 onions, peeled and sliced, 1 orange, sliced with its skin on, 4 or 5 whole hard pears, peeled, 4 whole allspice, 8 black peppercorns, some salt and 4 tablespoons of very best sherry vinegar (wine vinegar could be used but is nothing like so good). Add a 4½ lb (2.25 kg) chicken, cover and cook for 1 hour.

To finish, transfer chicken and pears to a warm serving dish, skim off fat from casserole and add 6 tablespoons stock and 6 tablespoons medium sherry. Boil hard for 2 to 3 minutes, then strain into a gravy dish. Serve with the chicken and pears.

As soon as the buds begin to burst in the spring,
the Pear suckers leave their winter quarters.
(1882)

Quail with Pears

Quail are delicately flavoured, as are pears,
so the two complement each other well.

¼ oz (7 g) butter per quail
1 plump quail per person
*few drops of onion juice (from a piece of
onion in a garlic press)*
few fresh pear slices, to garnish

SAUCE (for 4)
1 oz (30 g) butter
*1 in (2.5 cm) piece from white part of leek,
thinly sliced*
2–3 pears, skins left on, roughly chopped
2½ in (5 cm) piece cinnamon stick
4 fl oz (125 ml) port plus 1 tablespoon
2 teaspoons lemon juice
salt and pepper, to taste

Melt butter in a flameproof casserole, add
quail and onion juice and brown gently all

over, 7 to 10 minutes. Cover and pot roast for a further 7 to 10 minutes or until just cooked – quail become very dry if overcooked.

To make sauce, melt butter in a saucepan, add leek and pears and stir-fry for 4 to 5 minutes, then add cinnamon and 4 fl oz (125 ml) port, cover tightly and simmer for 15 to 20 minutes until very tender. Transfer to a blender or food processor and purée, then return to pan, add lemon juice, salt and pepper and reheat. Stir in remaining port and serve with quail.

Pear & Hazelnut Pudding

This recipe will use up some of the pear purée frozen earlier in the season. Two lb (1 kg) pears will make 20 fl oz (625 ml) thick purée.

Serves 5–6

20 fl oz (625 ml) pear purée, see page 89

2 tablespoons sugar

TOPPING

2 egg whites

4 oz (125 g) caster sugar

2 oz (60 g) toasted hazelnuts (see page 87), coarsely ground

Butter a pie dish. Mix together pear purée and sugar and pour into dish.

To make the topping, beat egg whites until stiff, then beat in caster sugar, a little at a time, and fold in hazelnuts. Spoon meringue mixture over pears, spreading to the edges of the dish and making peaks with a fork. Bake in a cool oven at 140 °C (275 °F/Gas 1) for 1½ to 2 hours.

A quicker cooking method is to bake in a moderately hot oven at 190 °C (375 °F/Gas 5) for 30 to 40 minutes. This gives a softer meringue topping similar to that on a lemon meringue pie.

Peare-Wardons are of all sorts of Peares the best and wholsomest.

(1866, Treas. Bot.)

Pear Clafoutis

A classic French dessert usually made with cherries but excellent with pears.

Serves 6
4–6 pears, according to size
2 tablespoons orange juice
3 oz. (90 g) plain flour, sifted
3 eggs, beaten
3 oz (90 g) sugar
10–12 fl oz (315–375 ml) milk
2 teaspoons caster sugar
2 teaspoons grated orange peel

Peel, core and halve pears and cover all over with orange juice. Place flour in a mixing bowl and beat in eggs, sugar and milk to give a thick, smooth pancake batter. Alternatively, process to a batter in a food processor.

Butter a shallow, ovenproof dish liberally, then put in the pears, core side down and pour over batter. Bake in a moderate oven, at 190 °C (375 °F/Gas 5) for 30 to 40 minutes, until risen and brown on top. Mix caster sugar and orange peel together, sprinkle over top and serve at once.

Pear & Chestnut Compote

Pears and nuts go well together. Walnuts and hazelnuts are popular but this quick and simple dessert with chestnuts is especially good. You will need one 14 oz (440 g) tin of chestnuts or chestnut pieces in heavy syrup and one fine, ripe pear per person. Peel, core and quarter the pears. Place in individual serving dishes and spoon over a tablespoon of chestnuts and their syrup. Drizzle over a little double (heavy) cream and finish with a dusting of finely grated plain dark chocolate.

As crest-falne as a dride-peare.
  (1598, Shakespeare, Merry Wives of Windsor)

Stuffed Pears in Hot Chocolate Sauce

Serves 4

4 pears
4 tablespoons cake crumbs
2 tablespoons raspberry jam
1 tablespoon brandy
4 oz (125 g) plain dark chocolate
1 tablespoon grated chocolate, to decorate

Peel, halve and core pears. Poach as in the recipe for 'Pear & Vanilla Compote', page 79, then remove from pan with a slotted spoon and leave to cool, reserving poaching liquor. Mix cake crumbs, jam and brandy together in a small bowl, then use to stuff pears. Arrange pear halves on a shallow serving dish and chill while preparing sauce.

Bring 6 fl oz (185 ml) poaching liquor to the boil in a small saucepan and boil hard for 4 to 5 minutes until liquid is reduced and slightly syrupy. Remove from heat and stir in chocolate. Leave to dissolve, then stir again and leave to cool slightly.

To serve, dust chilled pears with grated chocolate and pour round the hot chocolate sauce.

Stuffed Pears & Crème Pâtissière

This takes a little more trouble to make than 'Stuffed Pears & Hot Chocolate Sauce' but is so delicious that it is well worth the effort. It also looks very pretty. The crème pâtissière can be made 2 to 3 days in advance, covered and kept in the fridge.

Serves 4

4 dessert pears

CREME PATISSIERE
1 heaped teaspoon cornflour
5 fl oz (155 ml) milk
2 oz (60 g) sugar
2 egg yolks, beaten
4 oz (125 g) unsalted butter
vanilla extract, to taste

TO FINISH
4 tablespoons cake crumbs
2 tablespoons apricot jam
4 teaspoons Amaretto liqueur
4 teaspoons chopped almonds or biscuit crumbs
angelica or mint leaves

Keeping fruit whole, remove cores from pears, working from the base and stopping before you reach the top end. Do not break through and, if possible, leave stalk attached as this looks pretty in the finished dish. To do this it is easiest to start with a vegetable peeler, then use a teaspoon to scoop out a medium-sized hole for the stuffing. Once cored, peel and poach as in the recipe for 'Pear & Vanilla Compote', page 79. Remove from pan and leave to cool.

To make the crème pâtissière, blend cornflour with milk in a bowl until smooth, then pour into a saucepan, add sugar and egg yolks and cook gently over a low heat, stirring all the time until mixture thickens and becomes smooth. Bring just to the boil to cook the cornflour, then remove from heat and beat hard. Leave to cool, stirring occasionally. When almost cold, beat in butter, a knob at a time, then beat in vanilla and leave to cool completely.

To assemble, place a teaspoon of crème pâtissière for each pear in the bottom of a small, deep, straight-sided serving dish (which will just take the pears), or use individual dishes. Mix together cake crumbs and jam and use to stuff pears, then stand pears upright on top of cream in serving dish. Pack closely together or they will not stay upright.

Serve with a teaspoon of liqueur and a dusting of nuts or biscuit crumbs over each pear and decorate with angelica or mint.

Pear & Honey Layer Cake

This cake is a cross between a sponge cake and a shortbread. It is filled with a layer of buttered pears and can be eaten hot, warm or cold. It will keep for 4 to 5 days but is really at its best a day old.

Serves 6
2 oz (60 g) butter
1 lb (500 g) pears, peeled, cored and sliced
1 oz (30 g) sugar

DOUGH
4 oz (125 g) butter
2 oz (60 g) honey
2 eggs
2 tablespoons Greek-style yogurt
10–12 oz (315–375 g) self-raising flour

ICING
juice of 1/2 orange
8 oz (250 g) icing sugar
2 teaspoons orange flower water

Melt butter in a saucepan with a tight-fitting lid, add pears and sugar, cover and simmer until tender, 10 to 15 minutes. Leave to cool in juices.

To make the dough, cream butter and honey together in a bowl, then beat in eggs one at a time. Add yogurt and beat again, then carefully fold in flour. The mixture should be firm enough to shape with the hands or gently roll – stickier than pastry dough but not as wet as scone dough.

Butter a 9 in (22.5 cm) deep fruit cake tin well. Divide dough into two, roll into balls and pat out to fit cake tin. Press one of the dough circles into the tin, working dough up the sides to make a shallow shell to hold the pears. Carefully spoon in cooled pears and juice, place second dough circle on top and press edges gently together. Bake at 190 °C (375 °F/Gas 5) for 30 to 40 minutes or until deep golden brown on top.

Meanwhile make the icing. Heat orange juice in a saucepan, add icing sugar and bring to the boil. Boil for 1 minute, then stir in orange flower water. Pour over cake while it is still hot.

If not eating hot, leave to cool in tin.

Peares are muche of the nature of appulles, but they ar heuier.

(1533, Elyot)

Pears in Maple Syrup

Not a formal pudding but a useful and quick way of turning ripe eating pears into an unusual dessert. Maple syrup is available at most supermarkets.

For each person you will need one ripe pear, peeled, cored and sliced. Place in a bowl, pour over one tablespoon of best quality maple syrup and toss gently. Thick cream or plain yogurt or a mixture of both in equal portions is good served with this dish and orange slices make a pretty decoration.

Pear & Vanilla Compote

This is a perfect dish, simple and elegant. Good pears and real vanilla – not essence – have a natural affinity.

Serves 8

8 dessert pears
30 fl oz (940 ml) water
1 vanilla pod
4 oz (125 g) sugar
vanilla biscuits or sponge fingers, to serve

Peel, core and halve pears, reserving peelings. Drop pears straightaway into a bowl of lightly salted water to prevent them from turning brown. Pour 30 fl oz (940 ml) water into a saucepan, add vanilla pod and reserved pear peelings, bring to the boil and simmer for 30 to 45 minutes. Remove vanilla pod and reserve, then strain off liquid into a clean shallow pan. Add sugar and dissolve. Pat pear halves dry on absorbent kitchen paper and cook in pan a few at a time until tender, 7 to 10 minutes depending on type and ripeness of pear. Using a slotted spoon, transfer to serving bowl. When all pear halves are cooked increase the heat and boil juice fast, until reduced to a light syrup. Pour over fruit and chill. Serve with vanilla biscuits or sponge fingers. Cream would spoil the delicate flavour of this dish.

Pear Sorbet

This quick and simple recipe can easily be made with frozen pear purée, see page 89. The better the pears, the better the flavour. To every 20 fl oz (625 ml) thick unsweetened pear purée (thawed if frozen) you will need 1 egg white, 2 oz (60 g) caster sugar and your chosen flavouring: vanilla is good, so is orange zest or ground cinnamon. You may like to add a few drops of edible green food colouring to the purée.

The method is simple: beat the egg white until stiff, then add sugar a little at a time, beating well in between. Add flavouring and gently fold in the pear purée. Pour into freezing container, cover and freeze.

Pear Preserve
A delicious jam from Bavaria, Germany.

*4 lb (2 kg) pears, peeled and cored, see
method*
1 1/2 oz (45 g) butter
juice of 1 orange
3 lb (1.5 kg) sugar
2 tablespoons white wine vinegar

Save pear peelings and cores and tie in a
piece of muslin. Melt butter and orange juice
in a preserving pan, add pears, roughly
chopped, and cook together over a low heat
for 5–10 minutes. Add peel and cores in the
muslin together with sugar and stir until dissolved. Cook for 1–1½ hours, stirring occasionally to prevent sticking. Stir in vinegar
and cook for a further 10 to 15 minutes. Pour
into sterilized jars and pot, see page 87.

Plain Shortcrust Pastry

Suitable for savoury and sweet tarts.

8 oz (250 g) flour
½ teaspoon salt
4 oz (125 g) butter or margarine, hard and cold
3–4 tablespoons ice-cold water

Sift flour and salt into a mixing bowl. Cut fat into flour using two knives or a pastry cutter and mix briefly in a food processor or rub in with fingertips. When mixture looks like breadcrumbs, add water and draw together; the mixture should be very stiff. Knead together against the sides of the bowl, then wrap in plastic wrap and leave in a cool place or the bottom of the fridge for 30 minutes or until you wish to use it. If left for several hours or overnight, the pastry should be brought to room temperature for 2 to 3 hours before use.

Rough Puff Pastry

An alternative to puff pastry: use for sweet or savoury dishes.

8 oz (250 g) flour
1/2 teaspoon salt
4 oz (125 g) butter
2 oz (60 g) lard
4–6 tablespoons ice-cold water

Sift flour and salt into a mixing bowl. Cut fats into flour using a knife – the pieces need not be very small. Make a well in the mixture, add water and mix the dough to an elastic consistency.

Turn out on to a floured board and knead. Roll into a long strip, flour lightly, then fold in three and seal the edges with the rolling pin. Give the pastry a half turn, roll out again, flour again, fold and seal. Turn again and roll out a third time; the fat should now be evenly distributed, if not, roll out a fourth time. Fold again, wrap in plastic wrap and leave in a cool place or the fridge until needed.

Suet Pastry

8 oz (250 g) self-raising flour
good pinch salt
*4 oz (125 g) chopped suet or use butter if
you prefer*
2–4 tablespoons water

Sieve flour with salt into a mixing bowl, stir in suet and mix well. If using butter, rub into flour and salt until mixture resembles fine breadcrumbs. Add enough water to give a stiff paste, the dough should be moister than a normal pastry dough. Place on a floured board to roll out.

Pancakes

Makes about eight 7 in (17.5 cm) pancakes.

4 oz (125 g) plain flour
1 whole egg
1 egg yolk
3 tablespoons brandy
7–8 fl oz (220–250 ml) skimmed milk
good quality cooking oil

Sieve flour into a bowl and make a well in the centre. Add egg, egg yolk, brandy and milk, and, using a wire whisk or electric beater, beat well until mixture is smooth and light.

Leave to rest in a cold place for 30 minutes. The mixture can be left longer – any time up to 2 hours.

Pour 3 tablespoons cooking oil into a heavy-bottomed frying pan and swirl to coat, then pour off surplus oil. Heat oil, then pour in enough batter to give a very thin layer covering the bottom of the pan. Cook for 1–1½ minutes over a medium-hot heat lifting edges with a palette knife to check that pancake is not burning – it should be cream and golden when it is cooked. When ready, turn with the help of palette knife and cook other side. Remove and place on a warm plate. Cover with slightly damp absorbent kitchen paper and keep warm in a very low oven until ready to use. Make each pancake the same way, pouring off oil in between.

Oaks and beeches last longer than apples and pears.

(1626, Bacon)

To Toast Hazelnuts

Gently heat a clean, dry frying pan. When hot, add hazelnuts and cook until their skins begin to brown, shaking the pan occasionally to ensure even browning. Turn into a large wire sieve and rub off the skins. Turn out either on to a clean tea towel or 2 to 3 sheets of absorbent kitchen paper.

To Test Jam for Set

Remove saucepan or preserving pan from heat and put a little jam or jelly on to a cold plate. Leave to cool, then tilt the plate slightly. The jam is setting if it begins to wrinkle at this point.

If using a sugar thermometer, 'set' is reached at 110°C/220°F.

To Pot Jam, Curd or Preserves

Potting must be done correctly to keep food from developing bacteria.

Make sure that the jars are completely sterile, warm and dry. Remove any foam that may have formed on the surface of the jam and pot carefully and quickly. Fill jars to the brim, cover with wax circles, then seal with self-sealing lids. Label and store in a cool, dark place or the fridge, as directed.

*Go see what's doing in the cheese-chamber and
the apple-loft.*

(1740, Mrs Delaney, Autobiography)

Storing & Freezing

The old-fashioned way of storing was to lay
prime fruits out on clean paper on attic or loft
floor. This is still a good way to store cooking
or dessert apples if you can keep children
and mice away! Pears don't respond to this
treatment, they go 'dozy'.

Both apples and pears can be dried: apples
in rings and pears in halves. Peel, core and
slice apples into rings and string them up in
an airing cupboard. Peel, core and halve
pears. Cover baking sheets with absorbent
kitchen paper, lay out pears on top and leave
to dry out in a very, very cool oven.

Freezing does not, I think, suit either of
these fruits unless they are cooked. Apples
can be frozen if you peel, core and slice them,
blanch for 1 minute in boiling water, then
drain, cool and pack into plastic bags.
However, the end result of all this work is a
rather tasteless dish. Turning them into a
purée is the quickest and easiest way to deal
with a glut of apples for the freezer. Wash,
core and slice the apples, place in a saucepan
with a tight-fitting lid and add just enough
water to prevent them from burning – 2 to 3

tablespoons per 1 lb (500 g) fruit. Bring to the boil, cover and simmer for 20 to 30 minutes until soft and mushy, stirring occasionally during cooking to prevent burning and adding more water if necessary. Cool, then purée in a blender or food processor or pass through a sieve. Pack into boxes and freeze. It is better not to add sugar or flavouring at this stage but to do so after you have thawed the purée. The purée freezes well and retains a good flavour.

Baked apples also freeze well; next time you are baking apples, do several extra, then leave to cool, pack into containers and freeze. To serve, thaw at room temperature and reheat gently in the oven.

A cooked pear purée freezes well. Make it as for apples, but peel pears before cooking: 2 lb (1 kg) pears make 20 fl oz (625 ml) thick purée. Alternatively, you can slice them and cook them in a sugar syrup. As pears lose their flavour it is best to add flavouring to the syrup – thinly pared orange peel, vanilla pod or cinnamon stick are all good. 20 fl oz (625 ml) water and 6 oz (185 ml) sugar will poach 2 to 3 lb (1 to 1.5 kg) pears. Peel, core and halve pears and poach only a few at a time. Remove with a slotted spoon and pack into boxes, pour over the syrup, cover and freeze. The flavouring ingredients may be frozen with the fruit.

INDEX